BIBLE ABCs

By Marie A. Bailey

WTL INTERNATIONAL

Bible ABCs

Copyright © 2021 Marie A. Bailey

Images created by: Canva, Richard Gunther, 123RF.com artists, and Cutie Fruity courtesy of Aisha Hammah:
Front cover: Canva; Adam: Canva and Danilo Sanino @ 123RF.com; Bethlehem: grgroup @ 123RF.com;
Cross: yupiramos @ 123RF.com; David: tomaccojc @ 123RF.com;
Esther: Aisha Hammah and Canva; Faith: Canva; Grace: Canva; Heaven: Danilo Sanino @ 123RF.com;
Isaac: Aisha Hammah and jiiiikkk @ Fiverr.com; Jesus: Hong Li @ 123RF.com and jakkapan @ 123RF.com;
Kindness: Evgenii Naumov @ 123RF.com; Lazarus: Richard Gunther; Moses: tomaccojc @ 123RF.com;
Noah: siberianart @ 123RF.com; Offering: Aisha Hammah and Andrii Sorii @ 123RF.com; Peter: grgroup @ 123RF.com;
Quail: Aisha Hammah; Rahab: Aisha Hammah; Solomon: Aisha Hammah and Christos Georghiou @ 123RF.com;
Thomas: grgroup @ 123RF.com; Urim: Aisha Hammah; Vow: Aisha Hammah; Water: Aisha Hammah; Xerxes:
Tetiana Lazunova @ 123RF.com; Youth: Evgenii Naumov @ 123RF.com;
Zacharias: Maryna Kriuchenko @ 123RF.com

All rights reserved. No part of this publication may be reproduced
in any form or by any electronic or mechanical means, including information storage and material systems,
except in the case of brief quotations embodied in critical articles or reviews, without permission
in writing from its publisher,
WTL International.

Published by
WTL International
930 North Park Drive
P.O. Box 33049
Brampton, Ontario
L6S 6A7 Canada
www.wtlipublishing.com

978-1-927865-86-6

Printed in the U.S.A.

Introduction

This book was written, not necessarily to teach children the letters of the alphabet, but to introduce them to Bible places, characters and teachings associated with each letter. The book can be used as a springboard for telling Bible stories to young ones. I have made reference to specific places in the Bible where the words are used, the stories related to them are told, or where the characters are mentioned. This feature will help parents, teachers or older readers to locate the relevant Bible passages. Most references are from the New King James Version (NKJV) of the Bible but I also used the New International Version (NIV) and the New Living Translation (NLT). A Bible Concordance can be used to find other references.

Children as old as eight or ten years old can benefit from this book as some of the stories and concepts will best be understood by a more mature audience. A child could receive the book as a toddler but cherish it for many years as he or she learns more about the various Bible characters and their place in Bible history. Eventually, the child will read the stories or accounts for himself or herself without the aid of an adult. The book can also be a great resource for Bible trivia for young children.

It is my hope that Bible ABCs will introduce children to, and open the door for even more to be learned about and from the Bible, the greatest book ever written.

Dedication

This book is dedicated to all the children of the world: red, brown, yellow, black and white. You are precious in God's sight and He loves you. In fact, Jesus said in Matthew 19 verse 14, "Let the children come to me. Don't stop them! For the kingdom of Heaven belongs to such as these." Then He put His hands on their heads and blessed them...verse 15 (NLT).

May you be blessed as you read this book and may it inspire you to read the entire Bible, on which it is based.

Acknowledgements

I must, first of all give thanks and praise to my Heavenly Father and the Lord Jesus who drew me to themselves and from whom came the knowledge and wisdom to create this work. I have loved reading the Bible since my childhood and I am thankful that God helped me get a good education so I can read, understand and share His word.

My husband, Dereck, also deserves some credit. He has always encouraged me to write even when I doubted that I could be successful at writing, and was willing to invest financially in the project at tremendous personal sacrifice.

To the friends, especially Barbara Collash, Claire Green and Dorrett Homer, who supported my decision to have the book published, I say thanks for believing in me. Claire and Barbara also made helpful suggestions when changes needed to be made to the original script and illustrations.

To my siblings who were not only elated at the news that I had written a book and was having it published, but cheered me on during the process.

Mario Palmer, my nephew, did some of the artwork and generated the first ideas on how to illustrate the book. Thanks Mario.

Last, but not least, my thanks go out to Aisha of WTL International, my publisher. She loved the work from the onset and believed it could be a success. I appreciate all the sacrifices made on my behalf and the hard work and effort that went into getting the book published.

God bless you all.

A is for Adam – The Very First Man

(Genesis 1:26-27 Genesis 2:7-8)

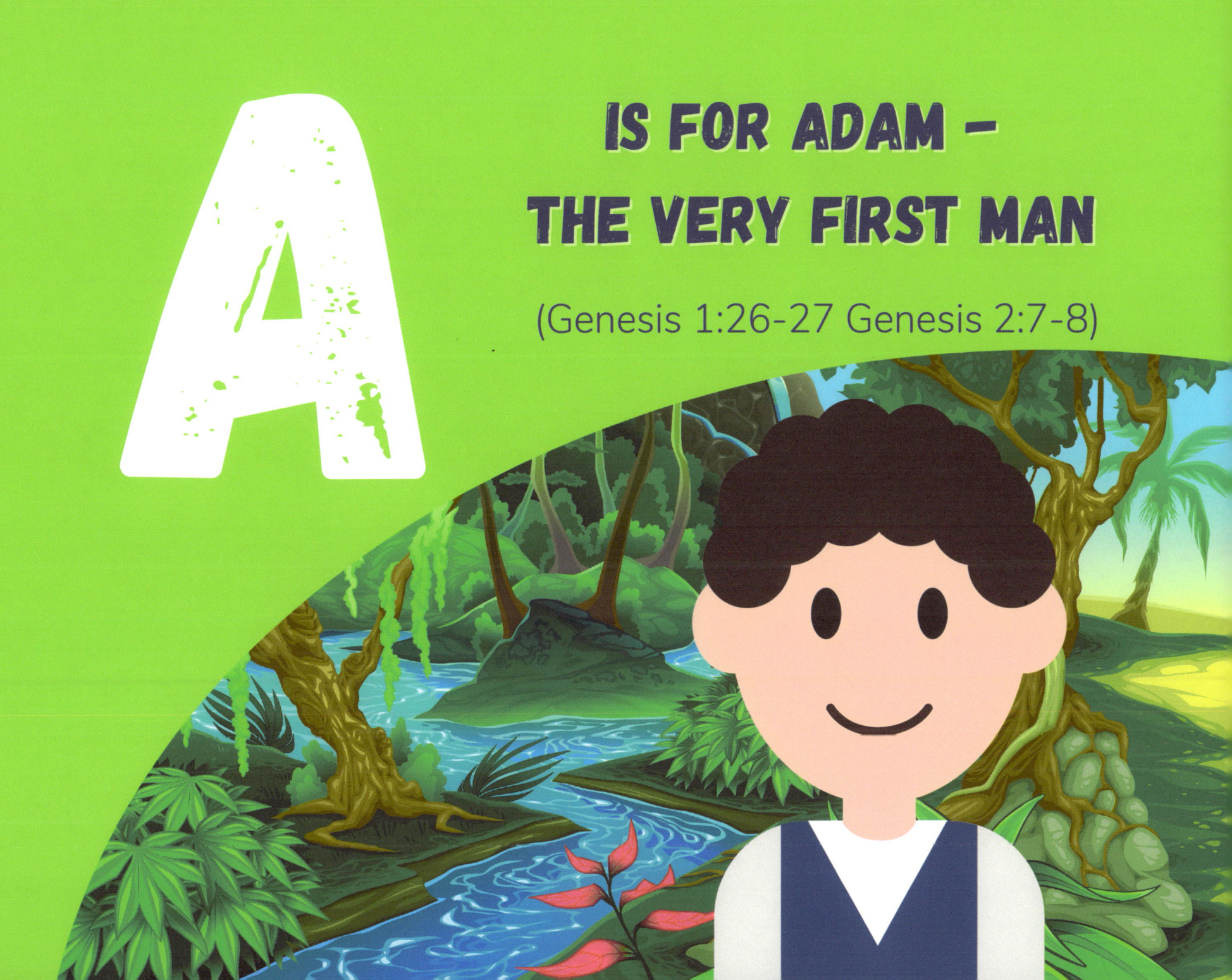

 **IS FOR BETHLEHEM – THE TOWN WHERE JESUS WAS BORN**

(Matthew 2:1; Luke 2:4-7)

C IS FOR THE CROSS ON WHICH JESUS DIED

(John 19:17-18)

 **IS FOR DAVID – HE KILLED GOLIATH WITH A SLING AND WROTE MOST OF THE PSALMS**

(1 Samuel 17)

 **IS FOR ESTHER – SHE RISKED HER LIFE TO SAVE HER PEOPLE**

(Esther 4:13-16)

 **IS FOR FAITH – WE NEED IT TO PLEASE GOD**

(Hebrews 11:6)

G IS FOR GRACE – BY WHICH WE ARE SAVED

(Ephesians 2:8)

H IS FOR HEAVEN – WHERE GOD LIVES

(Matthew 5:16; Matthew 6:9)

I IS FOR ISAAC – THE SON GOD GAVE TO ABRAHAM

(Genesis 17:19; Genesis 21:1-3)

J  IS FOR JESUS – HE DIED TO SAVE US FROM SIN

(Romans 5:8)

 **IS FOR KINDNESS – WHAT CHRIST WANTS US TO SHOW EACH OTHER**

(Ephesians 4:32)

 **IS FOR LAZARUS – JESUS RAISED HIM FROM THE DEAD**

(John 11:1-44)

M IS FOR MOSES – GOD GAVE HIM THE TEN COMMANDMENTS

(Exodus 31:18; Exodus 32:15-16)

N IS FOR NOAH – GOD TOLD HIM TO BUILD AN ARK

(Genesis 6:9-22)

O IS FOR OFFERING – WE SHOULD OFFER OUR BEST TO GOD

(Genesis 4:3-5; 2 Corinthians 9:7)

Time
Talent
Treasure

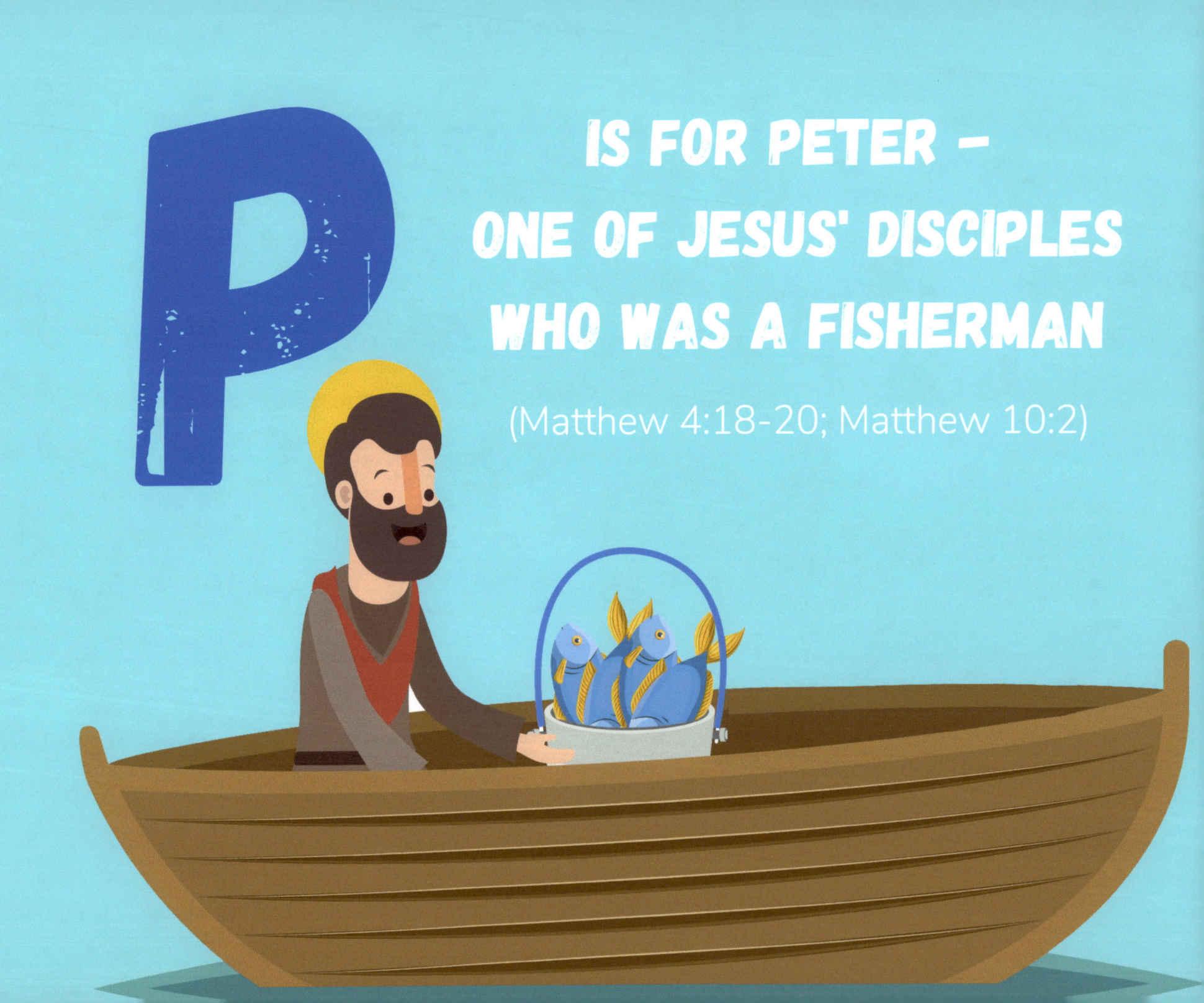

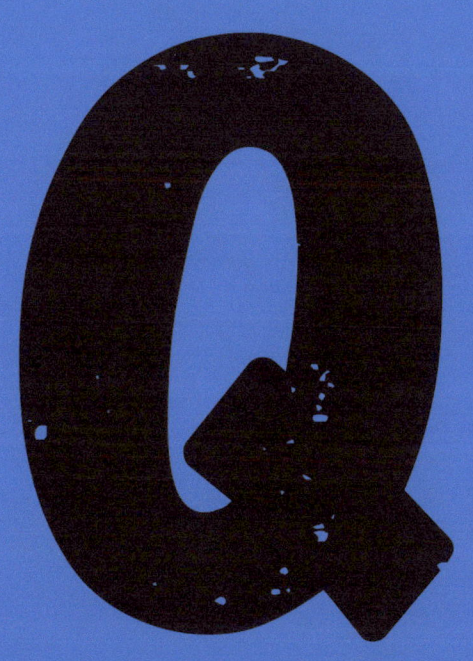

Q IS FOR QUAILS – GOD FED THE ISRAELITES WITH THEM

(Numbers 11:1-23; Numbers 11:31-34)

IS FOR RAHAB – SHE HID THE SPIES IN JERICHO

(Joshua 2:1-24)

# S IS FOR SOLOMON – THE WISEST MAN WHO EVER LIVED

(1 Kings 3:12; 1 Kings 4:29-31)

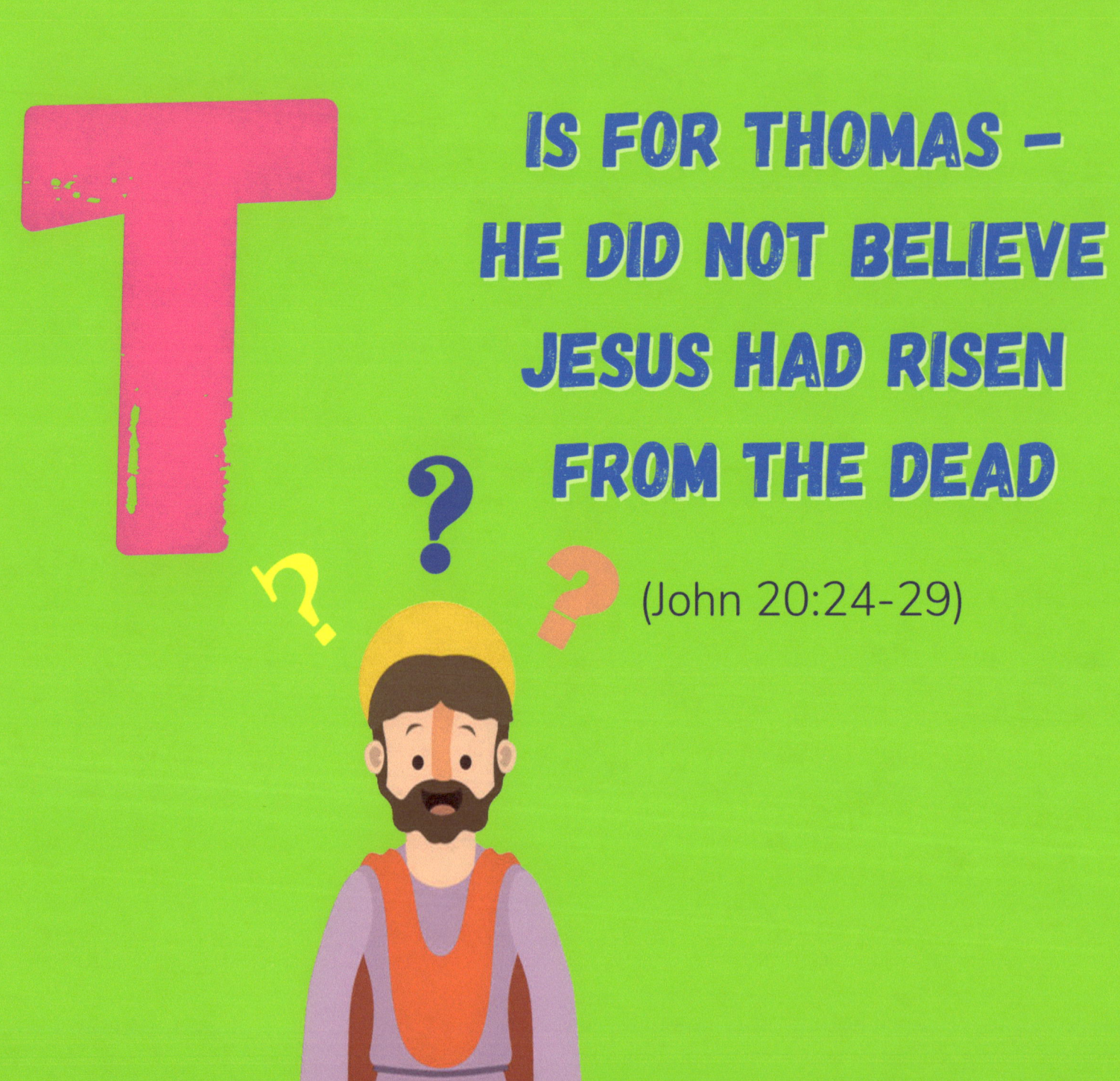

U IS FOR URIM –
WORN BY THE HIGH PRIEST WHEN INQUIRING OF GOD OR MAKING DECISIONS

(Exodus 28:30)

V IS FOR VOW – A PROMISE MADE TO GOD

(Genesis 28:20-22)

W

IS FOR WATER – JESUS TURNED IT INTO WINE

(John 2:1-11)

X  IS FOR XERXES – THE KING OF PERSIA WHO MADE ESTHER HIS QUEEN

(Esther 2:1-18 NIV)

Y IS FOR YOUTH – GOD WANTS US TO SERVE HIM WHILE WE ARE YOUNG

(Ecclesiastes 12:1)

Z IS FOR ZACHARIAS – THE FATHER OF JOHN THE BAPTIST WHO WAS OBEDIENT AND NAMED HIS SON JOHN

(Luke 1:5-25; Luke 1:57-66)

www.ingramcontent.com/pod-product-compliance
Lightning Source LLC
LaVergne TN
LVHW070908080426
835510LV00004B/124